REFLECTING FAMILIES

AN ANTHOLOGY OF POETRY

EDITED BY JUDITH CHERNAIK

Publishing Manager: Mina Patria
Commissioning Editor: Steve Pollock
Designer: XAB Design (Cover) and Maxine Fox

Published for the International Year of the Family 1994

First published in 1995 by BBC Educational Developments,
White City, 201 Wood Lane, London W12 7TS.

Typeset in Times
Printed by Borough Press, Wiltshire

ISBN 1 86000 105 X

*C*ontents

'Go to your
wide futures'

'Close-dancing families'

*F*rom our
colleagues

Foreword

This anthology celebrates the end of the International Year of the Family in 1994. Four charities joined with BBC Education to make this project happen. The National Early Years Network, Exploring Parenthood and Help the Aged in the UK, and Age and Opportunity in Ireland, all support work with people in different stages of family life, from infancy through to old age.

Why choose a book of poetry to celebrate the International Year of the Family? It seemed to us that while families occupy so much of our time and fuel so many emotions, poems about them are few and far between. The day-to-day struggles and joys of parenthood, the way we change in relation to each other as we grow older, are so closely woven into our lives that they are easily overlooked.

To find the poems we canvassed more than a hundred poets and issued an invitation to members of the public through BBC Radio to suggest poems which meant something to them. One listener wrote in to say: 'Family is more than the sum of its parts. It manifests itself in a tiny gesture, a facial expression, a well-worn story, a look which flashes across the faces with different features, and binds people through their genes, across generations and beyond memory.' Such comments helped to shape
this anthology.

The project was supported by the European Commission and the anthology brings together reflections on family life from different parts of Europe. Besides poems from the United Kingdom and Ireland, poems from the Netherlands and Belgium have been specially translated into English. A Flemish/Dutch anthology has also been published in parallel and English language poems were translated for it from this collection.

We hope you will enjoy reading this anthology and will be taken on the odd unexpected journey. Family relationships, with all their joys and problems, go on for generations; we hope *Reflecting Families* will do the same.

Introduction

There is a special pleasure in editing a collection of poems which is a true collaboration between writers and readers.

Over a hundred poets from all parts of the UK and Eire sent us their own choice of poems about family life, and these tended to be intensely personal — about a child's birth, a parent's death, sibling affection and rivalry, and all the changing phases of love and marriage. Readers and radio listeners sent in family favourites by Burns and Hardy, Seamus Heaney and Roger McGough. Patrick Kavanagh's moving elegies for his mother and father were popular choices among Irish poetry lovers, as was Yeats's love poem 'When You Are Old'. Friends and relatives suggested poems reflecting their own family circumstances — as good a test of relevance as any.

Although well-loved sonnets by Shakespeare and Elizabeth Barrett Browning have a natural place here, it seems right for an anthology reflecting contemporary family life to concentrate on living poets. Many of these poems celebrate family relationships. Others deal with separation, loss and death; and the stresses and strains of generational conflict appear in a number of poems.

We tried to strike a balance between realism and nostalgia, and to include a wide range of experience, reflecting the diversity of family relations in our time. But our chief care was to choose poems which touch a chord of recognition and speak to the heart. These poems are full of feeling, but the predominant sentiment is love — love between parent and child, between partners, between the very young and the very old. In all, it is a reassuring collection, cutting across many times and cultures, and offering more than a grain of hope for the future.

Judith Chernaik

'I am the family face'

Heredity

I am the family face;
Flesh perishes, I live on,
Projecting trait and trace
Through time to times anon,
And leaping from place to place
Over oblivion.

The years-heired feature that can
In curve and voice and eye
Despise the human span
Of durance — that is I;
The eternal thing in man,
That heeds no call to die.

Thomas Hardy

The Cord

The little creature flies
or floats in the liberties
of its mother's body,
kicking from side to side of
its narrow round-edged pool
like a fish, or a kite that tries
the depth of its small warm sky
with a thoughtful pull
at the end of its tether,
the line that goes to earth.

If anything breaks that line
you can float free, down
an automatic wind
with freedom to fall to the end;
but if you survive, always
you will need to find the like
again, a string of looks
that tethers you to a face,
to the curve from which you depend,
to the dry warmth of a hand.

Alistair Elliot

The Sari

Inside my mother
I peered through a glass porthole.
The world beyond was hot and brown.

They were all looking in on me —
Father, Grandmother,
the cook's boy, the sweeper-girl,
the bullock with the sharp
shoulderblades,
the local politicians.

My English grandmother
took a telescope
and gazed across continents.

All the people unravelled a sari.
It stretched from Lahore to Hyderabad,
wavered across the Arabian Sea,
shot through with stars,
fluttering with sparrows and quails.
They threaded it with roads,
undulations of land.

Eventually
they wrapped and wrapped me in it
whispering *Your body is your country*.

Moniza Alvi

from
Frost at Midnight

The Frost performs its secret ministry,
Unhelped by any wind. The owlet's cry
Came loud — and hark, again! loud as before.
The inmates of my cottage, all at rest,
Have left me to that solitude, which suits
Abstruser musings: save that at my side
My cradled infant slumbers peacefully.

. . .

  Dear Babe, that sleepest cradled by my side,
Whose gentle breathings, heard in this deep calm,
Fill up the interspersèd vacancies
And momentary pauses of the thought!
My babe so beautiful! it thrills my heart
With tender gladness, thus to look at thee,
And think that thou shalt learn far other lore,
And in far other scenes! For I was reared
In the great city, pent 'mid cloisters dim,
And saw nought lovely but the sky and stars.
But thou, my babe! shalt wander like a breeze
By lakes and sandy shores, beneath the crags
Of ancient mountain, and beneath the clouds,
Which image in their bulk both lakes and shores
And mountain crags: so shalt thou see and hear
The lovely shapes and sounds intelligible
Of that eternal language, which thy God
Utters, who from eternity doth teach
Himself in all, and all things in himself.
Great universal Teacher! he shall mould
Thy spirit, and by giving make it ask.

Samuel Taylor Coleridge

Balloon

to Max and Jane

We took the children on the lake.

Wings like heartbeats, a stretched neck
Skimming over hazy water
Between an island and an island:
A wildfowl flying, black with distance.

Then a balloon, another bounty,
Hung with slung basket low above
A wooded bight, a stony bay,
Drifted like an hour hand
Across the flat and sunlit face
Of the lake, both motionless.

Yes, they will remember this;
And as I did, when young as they,
Think what is given us to see
Has always been, will always be;
Heretofore as hereafter
A duck flying, a balloon
Suspended with two people in
Its basket over Derwentwater.

David Wright

I Am Becoming My Mother

Yellow/brown woman
fingers smelling always of onions

My mother raises rare blooms
and waters them with tea
her birth waters sang like rivers
my mother is now me

My mother had a linen dress
the colour of the sky
and stored lace and damask
tablecloths
to pull shame out of her eye.

I am becoming my mother
brown/yellow woman
fingers smelling always of onions.

Lorna Goodison

Imitations

In this house, in this afternoon room,
my son and I. The other side of glass
snowflakes whitewash the shed roof and the grass
this surprised April. My son is sixteen,
an approximate man. He is my chameleon,
my soft diamond, my deciduous evergreen.

Eyes half closed he listens to pop forgeries
of music — how hard it is to know — and perhaps
dreams of some school Juliet I don't know.
Meanwhile, beyond the bending window,
gusting suddenly, despite a sky half blue,
a blur of white blossom, whiter snow.

And I stare, oh immortal springtime, till
I'm elsewhere and the age my cool son is,
my father alive again (I, his duplicate),
his high breath, my low breath, sticking to the glass
while two white butterflies stumble, held each
to each as if by elastic, and pass.

Dannie Abse

Mr Zweigenthal

He was your other father, she said,
awkwardly. I was lucky to have
two fathers, I thought, but he was
a secret; left behind a bow-tie
like a black malevolent butterfly,
a looped violin string, an address
in Danzig, a baby in her bed.

Played beautiful he did, at the end
of the pier, the August sun dipping
slowly into the sea, the turnstile
creaking as they ran home, laughing,
sliding on shingle, clutching stones
and shells, but careful with his fiddle
and the black suit she used to mend.

What did he think, I asked, my real dad,
when he came home from India and found me
sleeping in the crib beside her?
Wasn't he pleased? Her face grew
cracked all over. The lodger, a Jew,
it wasn't meant . . . a mistake, the pills
didn't work. I felt so bad, so bad.

Mr Zweigenthal, I have your nose,
your hands, but no talent for a waltz,
a barcarolle. I know you almost as well
as I know myself, with your dark moods,
and your tall stooping figure which broods
over my whole life, looking out across
the Baltic, and in your buttonhole a rose.

Elizabeth Bartlett

Nana Krishie the Midwife

So keen on me those old eyes
the tracked black face
flowed with light

The tongue and gum ladled
stubborn words remembering
how I the boy child had knocked
thirty years before and hustled her
to come to the little cottage

Come with owl's wisdom and red
calico bag of tricks
to end labour: snap
and smack a newborn to cry

And now she looked at me surprised
and not at all surprised I had
come back from abroad
looking in a widened range
out of miracles she used and knew
time had discredited

For her ancestor's knack
her tabooed secrets now worked
in books of others
as ancient practices

Dreaming in her illiterate life
I felt the faltering tones
her startling shivered voice
thanking God
for showing me ever so well

James Berry

Making Poems

A mother takes morning tea to her family;
she's not a drudge, she understands
how getting out of bed is hard
even when the floor is carpeted.

As we wake from dreams of a deep wood
where lost children look for pebbles
without a moon, the way
the curtains are drawn for us matters
if we're to be reconciled to the day.

We are the poems that we make
our voices give them life
our sounds are echoed
and words return to us with love.
By this we grow

and learn to light candles for each other —
markers for a long walk in the dark.

Cicely Herbert

Writing

I am writing poems
on a May morning
on the back of my son's drawings.

Or is it that he has drawn pictures
on the back of my scribbles?

Anyway, my words are warmer
for his backing.

Anne Le Marquand Hartigan

To My Daughter

'Families,' I said, conscious that I could not find
  The adequate epithet, 'are nice.'
'Nice families,' you replied, adding
  To the faded adjective a tiny spice,
'Are nice.' What I had meant was this:
  How far we (a wandering family) have come
Since that day I backpacked you down
  Into an Arizona canyon with its river
Idling below us, broad and slow;
  Next, it was the steady Susquehanna;
Now swifter currents of the Severn show
  That time is never at a stand, although the daughter
You are leading by the hand, to me
  Seems that same child cradled in Arizona.
No — you are right —: *nice* will never do:
  But it is only families can review
Time in this way — the ties of blood
  Rooting us in place, not like the unmoving trees,
And yet, as subject to earth, water, time
  As they, our stay and story linked in rhyme.

Charles Tomlinson

Follower

My father worked with a horse-plough,
His shoulders globed like a full sail strung
Between the shafts and the furrow.
The horses strained at his clicking tongue.

An expert. He would set the wing
And fit the bright steel-pointed sock.
The sod rolled over without breaking.
At the headrig, with a single pluck

Of reins, the sweating team turned round
And back into the land. His eye
Narrowed and angled at the ground,
Mapping the furrow exactly.

I stumbled in his hob-nailed wake,
Fell sometimes on the polished sod;
Sometimes he rode me on his back
Dipping and rising to his plod.

I wanted to grow up and plough,
To close one eye, stiffen my arm.
All I ever did was follow
In his broad shadow round the farm.

I was a nuisance, tripping, falling,
Yapping always. But today
It is my father who keeps stumbling
Behind me, and will not go away.

Seamus Heaney

Background Material

My writing desk. Two photos, mam and dad.
A birthday, him. Their ruby wedding, her.
Neither one a couple and both bad.
I make out what's behind them from the blur.

Dad's in our favourite pub, now gone for good.
My father and his background are both gone,
but hers has my Welsh cottage and a wood
that still shows those same greens eight summers on,
though only the greenness of it 's stayed the same.

Though one of them 's in colour and one 's not,
the two are joined, apart from their shared frame,
by what, for photographers, would mar each shot:

in his, if you look close, the gleam, the light,
me in his blind right eye, but minute size —

in hers, as though just cast from where I write,
a shadow holding something to its eyes.

Tony Harrison

This Be The Verse

They fuck you up, your mum and dad,
    They may not mean to, but they do.
They fill you with the faults they had
    And add some extra, just for you.

But they were fucked up in their turn
    By fools in old-style hats and coats,
Who half the time were soppy-stern
    And half at one another's throats.

Man hands on misery to man.
    It deepens like a coastal shelf.
Get out as early as you can,
    And don't have any kids yourself.

Philip Larkin

Holotropic Botanicus

I close my eyes to find before me
A wooden door with a silver handle
Which I feel unable to open
Which opens by itself inwardly

Beyond it a blackscape of stars
Weakens down to the glimmer
Of a sweating pane of glass
Curved within corroding girders

The Waterlily house of the Botanic Gardens
My son's face moistened in the sultry light
We are seated by the plopping waterwheel
And we are smiling across at each other

I only realise as the scene is dissipating
That I am him and the tall figure my mother
Goldfish flit through the green water
And we are smiling across at each other

Dermot Bolger

Make Believe

Say I were not sixty,
say you weren't near-hundred,
say you were alive.
Say my verse was read
in some distant country,
and say you were idly turning the pages:

The blood washed from your shirt,
the tears from your eyes,
the earth from your bones;
neither missing since 1940,
nor dead as reported later
by a friend of a friend of a friend . . .

Quite dapper you stand in that bookshop
and chance upon my clues.

That is why at sixty
when some publisher asks me
for biographical details,
I still carefully give
the year of my birth,
the name of my hometown:

GERDA MAYER born 1927, in Karlsbad,
Czechoslovakia ... write to me, father.

Gerda Mayer

Note: The author's father, Arnold Stein, escaped from the German
concentration camp in Nisko in 1939, fled to Russian-occupied
Lemberg/Lwow, and then disappeared in the summer of 1940. It is thought
he may have died in a Russian camp.

Going On

Scotch and water, warm,
Medicinal, two tablets
On a little tray, his *Times*
Tucked underarm, a dignified
But frail ascent, prolonged
Undressing measured out
By heavy footsteps, coughing
Gently not to worry us, as if
A mere polite reminder, then
The silence of the grave.

And why must I recall this now
As half-way up the stairs
I hear my grown son calling
Going on, then, Dad?
An early night? Sleep well.

John Mole

Request to a Year

If the year is meditating a suitable gift,
I should like it to be the attitude
of my great-great-grandmother,
legendary devotee of the arts,

who, having had eight children
and little opportunity for painting pictures,
sat one day on a high rock
beside a river in Switzerland

and from a difficult distance viewed
her second son, balanced on a small ice-floe,
drift down the current towards a waterfall
that struck rock-bottom eighty feet below,

while her second daughter, impeded,
no doubt, by the petticoats of the day,
stretched out a last-hope alpenstock
(which luckily later caught him on his way).

Nothing, it was evident, could be done;
and with the artist's isolating eye
my great-great-grandmother hastily sketched the scene.
The sketch survives to prove the story by.

Year, if you have no Mother's day present planned;
reach back and bring me the firmness of her hand.

Judith Wright

Seven Sea Interludes

I

Childhood is soft chalk: it allows the sea
To erode, almost to break through; were we
Forever children, there would be no Midlands,
Only sea air, a mirror-line of headlands.

II

Adolescence arrived like a storm beach
Overnight, with bodies, much sea-wrack, and each
Shingled face turning guiltily from salt
Ejaculations to identify a fault.

III

Student days hang like a pantomime horseshoe:
That bay on whose shores we held our barbecue —
Debate-cum-dance, loving the tides' motion;
Aware, of course, from lectures, of the pollution.

IV

As young couples we kiss to the cliff's edge,
Lie down with razorbills on a narrow ledge,
Laugh at the lifeguard, laugh at the fishing folk
In their corky craft, the sea is a huge joke.

V

Executive schedules seldom cover
The seaside; only if there's a lover
Or a business conference. One buys a yacht.
One moors it in Poole Harbour. The strakes rot.

VI

Parenthood is a final glimpse of the gold
You found on the beach as a one-year-old.
Return to the Landslip: the past gives way
And you are your children, have feet of clay.

VII

A Saga Holiday, perhaps. Promenades
Before supper, an evening playing cards.
Images in a land-locked single room
Of crossing the bar; stacks, arches; the blown spume.

John Greening

' Breathing in unison'

'Let me not to the marriage of true minds'

Let me not to the marriage of true minds
Admit impediments. Love is not love
Which alters when it alteration finds,
Or bends with the remover to remove.
O, no! it is an ever-fixèd mark
That looks on tempests and is never shaken;
It is the star to every wand'ring bark,
Whose worth's unknown, although his height be taken.
Love's not Time's fool, though rosy lips and cheeks
Within his bending sickle's compass come;
Love alters not with his brief hours and weeks,
But bears it out even to the edge of doom.
　　If this be error and upon me proved,
　　I never writ, nor no man ever loved.

William Shakespeare

'How do I love thee? Let me count the ways'

How do I love thee? Let me count the ways.
I love thee to the depth and breadth and height
My soul can reach, when feeling out of sight
For the ends of Being and ideal Grace.
I love thee to the level of everyday's
Most quiet need, by sun and candlelight.
I love thee freely, as men strive for Right;
I love thee purely, as they turn from Praise.
I love thee with the passion put to use
In my old griefs, and with my childhood's faith.
I love thee with a love I seemed to lose
With my lost saints,— I love thee with the breath,
Smiles, tears, of all my life! —and, if God choose,
I shall but love thee better after death.

Elizabeth Barrett Browning

Old Fashioned Wedding

It was for this they were made,
The great present of their childhood
Kept unopened, the hard rules obeyed
And the grudged honey of being good:
A pure reward,
Better for being stored,
And, reached at last, seeming like the sea
Stretching after a dream of ice toward
The edge of reluctance properly.

So that the stunned moment now
When talk falls in the bright marquee
Is an elevation of hope, the drinks a vow
Naming everything which is to be;
And after this
The subtly twinned kiss
To start a carnal journey, and the night
Offering shining emphasis
Like crystal gifts emboldening the light.

To which the cynical, caught up
In the flurry of guy ropes let down,
And crushed flowers in delicate cups,
Pay tribute as sexual clowns.
After this huge
Joke, a terrible deluge
The speeding innocents know nothing of,
Mad hours, silence, subterfuge
And all the dark expedients of love.

Peter Porter

The Underground

There we were in the vaulted tunnel running,
You in your going-away coat speeding ahead
And me, me then like a fleet god gaining
Upon you before you turned to a reed

Or some new white flower japped with crimson
As the coat flapped wild and button after button
Sprang off and fell in a trail
Between the Underground and the Albert Hall.

Honeymooning, moonlighting, late for the Proms,
Our echoes die in that corridor and now
I come as Hansel came on the moonlit stones
Retracing the path back, lifting the buttons

To end up in a draughty lamplit station
After the trains have gone, the wet track
Bared and tensed as I am, all attention
For your step following and damned if I look back.

Seamus Heaney

Habitation

Marriage is not
a house or even a tent

it is before that, and colder:

the edge of the forest, the edge
of the desert
                the unpainted stairs
at the back where we squat
outside, eating popcorn

the edge of the receding glacier

where painfully and with wonder
at having survived even
this far

we are learning to make fire

Margaret Atwood

The Marriage

They will fit, she thinks,
but only if her backbone
cuts exactly into his rib cage,
and only if his knees
dock exactly under her knees
and all four
agree on a common angle.

All would be well
if only
they could face each other.

Even as it is
there are compensations
for having to meet
nose to neck
chest to scapula
groin to rump
when they sleep.

They look, at least,
as if they were going
in the same direction.

Anne Stevenson

My Box

My box is made of golden oak,
my lover's gift to me.
He fitted hinges and a lock
of brass and a bright key.
He made it out of winter nights,
sanded and oiled and planed,
engraved inside the heavy lid
in brass, a golden tree.

In my box are twelve black books
where I have written down
how we have sanded, oiled and planed,
planted a garden, built a wall,
seen jays and goldcrests, rare red kites,
found the wild heartsease, drilled a well,
harvested apples and words and days
and planted a golden tree.

On an open shelf I keep my box.
Its key is in the lock.
I leave it there for you to read,
or them, when we are dead,
how everything is slowly made,
how slowly things made me,
a tree, a lover, words, a box,
books and a golden tree.

Gillian Clarke

And You, Helen

And you, Helen, what should I give you?
So many things I would give you
Had I an infinite great store
Offered me and I stood before
To choose. I would give you youth,
All kinds of loveliness and truth,
A clear eye as good as mine,
Lands, waters, flowers, wine,
As many children as your heart
Might wish for, a far better art
Than mine can be, all you have lost
Upon the travelling waters tossed,
Or given to me. If I could choose
Freely in that great treasure-house
Anything from any shelf,
I would give you back yourself,
And power to discriminate
What you want and want it not too late,
Many fair days free from care
And heart to enjoy both foul and fair,
And myself, too, if I could find
Where it lay hidden and it proved kind.

Edward Thomas

A Dedication to my Wife

To whom I owe the leaping delight
That quickens my senses in our wakingtime
And the rhythm that governs the repose of our sleepingtime,
        The breathing in unison

Of lovers whose bodies smell of each other
Who think the same thoughts without need of speech
And babble the same speech without need of meaning.

No peevish winter wind shall chill
No sullen tropic sun shall wither
The roses in the rose-garden which is ours and ours only

But this dedication is for others to read:
These are private words addressed to you in public.

T.S. Eliot

The Smell of Cake

I love the smell of cake in kitchens,
To stand in the heat of work and feel
The air warm as baked stones.
Dough clings to wooden spoons and bowls,
The worn edges of an old recipe book.
And your hair is powdered with flour,
Your palms smooth as a washed baking-board.
Above all, I love the finish when, together
Under the calendar that's months behind,
We swop spoons from a basin of cream and lick,
My beard flecked with it, your chin white,
And between us our son yelling for a lick,
And rising all around, the smell of rich, cooked cake.

Sean Dunne

The Letter

With B.E.F. June 10. Dear Wife,
(Oh blast this pencil. 'Ere, Bill, lend's a knife.)
I'm in the pink at present, dear.
I think the war will end this year.
We don't see much of them square-'eaded 'Uns.
We're out of harm's way, not bad fed.
I'm longing for a taste of your old buns.
(Say, Jimmie, spare's a bite of bread.)
There don't seem much to say just now.
(Yer what? Then don't, yer ruddy cow!
And give us back me cigarette!)
I'll soon be 'ome. You mustn't fret.
My feet's improvin', as I told you of.
We're out in rest now. Never fear.
(VRACH! By crumbs, but that was near.)
Mother might spare you half a sov.
Kiss Nell and Bert. When me and you —
(Eh? What the 'ell! Stand to? Stand to!
Jim, give's a hand with pack on, lad.
Guh! Christ! I'm hit. Take 'old. Aye, bad.
No, damn your iodine. Jim? 'Ere!
Write my old girl, Jim, there's a dear.)

Wilfred Owen
Note: B.E.F. = British Expeditionary Force

Love

Like starting on a pilgrimage,
stepping blithely out over the gunwale
hoping to waltz on water;

hands working inside one another's lives,
grasping the heart, for hold.
I heard their voices through the wall

like summer murmuring;
he brought her honeycombs
in wooden frames soft as the host,

a small, hard, ball of wax
stayed forever in her mouth
after the sweetness.

But in the photograph they are still
striding out together along the beach,
smiling, confident,

striding into the confusion
of their final months, their love
a bonding, dulled, unspoken,

they will disappear, exemplary, together,
as if the sea had swallowed them,
leave echoes of a low, ongoing, music.

John F. Deane

Love after Love

The time will come
when, with elation,
you will greet yourself arriving
at your own door, in your own mirror,
and each will smile at the other's welcome,

and say, sit here. Eat.
You will love again the stranger who was your self.
Give wine. Give bread. Give back your heart
to itself, to the stranger who has loved you

all your life, whom you ignored
for another, who knows you by heart.
Take down the love letters from the bookshelf,

the photographs, the desperate notes,
peel your own image from the mirror.
Sit. Feast on your life.

Derek Walcott

The Separation

'Why can't you live together?'
the boy asks. He bends
away from the woman.
His profile is rigid, tired.
It's so late at night and
all evening they've quarrelled
and sworn, flung blue
murder of threats,
useless. And
when she asks for
his real worries, not homework,
not school, not friends, he
in quiet asks.
She knows he knows her reply,
steely and more helpless than when
long ago he asked 'why
can't I?' and got
answered 'because you
can't.' 'Because we can't'
finally and finally she answers.

Judith Kazantzis

When You Are Old

When you are old and grey and full of sleep,
And nodding by the fire, take down this book,
And slowly read, and dream of the soft look
Your eyes had once, and of their shadows deep;

How many loved your moments of glad grace,
And loved your beauty with love false or true,
But one man loved the pilgrim soul in you,
And loved the sorrows of your changing face;

And bending down beside the glowing bars,
Murmur, a little sadly, how Love fled
And paced upon the mountains overhead
And hid his face amid a crowd of stars.

W.B. Yeats

John Anderson My Jo

John Anderson my jo, John,
  When we were first acquent;
Your locks were like the raven,
  Your bony brow was brent;
But now your brow is beld, John,
  Your locks are like the snaw;
But blessings on your frosty pow,
  John Anderson my jo.

John Anderson my jo, John,
  We clamb the hill the gither;
And mony a canty day, John,
  We've had wi' ane anither:
Now we maun totter down, John,
  And hand in hand we'll go;
And sleep the gither at the foot,
  John Anderson my jo.

Robert Burns

One Flesh

Lying apart now, each in a separate bed,
He with a book, keeping the light on late,
She like a girl dreaming of childhood,
All men elsewhere — it is as if they wait
Some new event: the book he holds unread,
Her eyes fixed on the shadows overhead.

Tossed up like flotsam from a former passion,
How cool they lie. They hardly ever touch,
Or if they do it is like a confession
Of having little feeling — or too much.
Chastity faces them, a destination
For which their whole lives were a preparation.

Strangely apart, yet strangely close together,
Silence between them like a thread to hold
And not wind in. And time itself's a feather
Touching them gently. Do they know they're old,
These two who are my father and my mother
Whose fire from which I came, has now grown cold?

Elizabeth Jennings

Requiescat In Pace

Poor Tom lay dying. Faithful at his side
His wife and helpmeet sat, a tireless nurse,
Fixing his dosage, watching, anxious-eyed,
His laboured breathing sink from bad to worse,
Wiping his fevered forehead. He, poor soul,
With aching conscience, tried in vain to pray;
Then hot, remorseful tears began to roll
Across his cheeks. 'There's something I must say:
I have deceived you, Peg my dear,' he said,
'With cousin Beattie and your sister Joan.
I've lain with both, here in this very bed.'
'Don't fret, my love,' his wife replied. 'I've known
For years.' He stared. 'You knew?' 'Of course I knew.
Why else, dear Tom, would I have poisoned you?'

Gerard Benson

Old Widowers

You can tell them, the old widowers,
chatting outside the supermarket,
then drifting apart as if they had
somewhere to go, but you know
they don't; they have all day,
the old widowers.

Their jackets don't quite sit straight;
their ties are the wrong colours.
No-one inspects them now
of a morning; they're their own men.
They've slipped their moorings;

outward bound under no orders,
troubled only with freedom,
they hug the coast;
hesitate; stare far out
where the light flings down
its gauntlet of distance.

Sheenagh Pugh

The Widower

'After you died, those friends of ours
Invited me to stay,
So I came here, beside the sea,
To watch the waves all day.
Everyone's kind, the weather's mild,
And I am well, but why
Should I live here alone, while you
Alone should have to die?

The dogs run races on the sands,
The children splash and play,
Our friends lie basking in the sun,
Sharing their holiday.
We eat, we talk, we watch TV,
But I would rather be
Asleep with you, than waking here
Beside the dazzling sea.'

Ruth Silcock

'6 Selfhood begins with a walking away'

Infant Joy

'I have no name:
I am but two days old.'
What shall I call thee?
'I happy am,
Joy is my name.'
Sweet joy befall thee!

Pretty joy!
Sweet joy but two days old,
Sweet joy I call thee;
Thou dost smile,
I sing the while —
Sweet joy befall thee!

Infant Sorrow

My mother groan'd! my father wept.
Into the dangerous world I leapt:
Helpless, naked, piping loud:
Like a fiend hid in a cloud.

Struggling in my father's hands,
Striving against my swadling bands,
Bound and weary I thought best
To sulk upon my mother's breast.

William Blake

Waiting

We have gathered together
The things you will need immediately
And set them on a table
By the bed you will be born in.
You have three drawers to your name
Of clothes for the first months.

I go from room to room. The house
Is waiting. Our hands are ready.
Even not yet knowing you
We love you; grateful
For how you have increased us; glad
We have it in us to put out new love.

David Constantine

Naming You

We have not snared you
with the net of a name
we have not tamed you

you are energy the one
word that is every word
the sound of the gong

come into the garden
and we will sing you
white stars green leaves

such spring-fever
the birds hop and cheep
around your sleepy head

the surge and shining
the rocking of tall trees
in the eager wind

who are you what are you
but the little sister
of this world around you

morning star and sparrow
bluebell smouldering
the attentive yew

but the dance of time
the argument of choice
fingers reach out

well the world can wait
we are disciples
and nothing is arbitrary

you are your own word
and cannot grow out of
a careless visitation

you declare yourself
smiling bubble-blower
your eyes gentian blue

lolling by the willow
your bald head askew
like a medieval saint

come home little sister
take your proper place
in this shining garden

dear daughter come home
come home we are here
and listening for your name

Kevin Crossley-Holland

Child

Your clear eye is the one absolutely beautiful thing.
I want to fill it with colour and ducks,
The zoo of the new

Whose names you meditate —
April snowdrop, Indian pipe,
Little

Stalk without wrinkle,
Pool in which images
Should be grand and classical

Not this troublous
Wringing of hands, this dark
Ceiling without a star.

Sylvia Plath

Night Feed

This is dawn.
Believe me
This is your season, little daughter.
The moment daisies open,
The hour mercurial rainwater
Makes a mirror for sparrows.
It's time we drowned our sorrows.

I tiptoe in.
I lift you up
Wriggling
In your rosy zipped sleeper.
Yes, this is the hour
For the early bird and me
When finder is keeper.

I crook the bottle.
How you suckle!
This is the best I can be,
Housewife
To this nursery
Where you hold on,
Dear life.

A silt of milk.
The last suck.
And now your eyes are open,
Birth-coloured and offended.
Earth wakes.
You go back to sleep.
The feed is ended.

Worms turn.
Stars go in.
Even the moon is losing face.
Poplars stilt for dawn
And we begin
The long fall from grace.

I tuck you in.

Eavan Boland

Death of a Son

(who died in a mental hospital aged one)

Something has ceased to come along with me.
Something like a person: something very like one.
    And there was no nobility in it
      Or anything like that.

    Something was there like a one year
Old house, dumb as stone. While the near buildings
    Sang like birds and laughed
      Understanding the pact

    They were to have with silence. But he
Neither sang nor laughed. He did not bless silence
    Like bread, with words.
      He did not forsake silence.

    But rather, like a house in mourning
Kept the eye turned in to watch the silence while
    The other houses like birds
      Sang around him.

And the breathing silence neither
Moved nor was still.

    I have seen stones: I have seen brick
But this house was made up of neither bricks nor stone
    But a house of flesh and blood
      With flesh of stone

    And bricks for blood. A house
Of stones and blood in breathing silence with the other
    Birds singing crazy on its chimneys.
      But this was silence,

This was something else, this was
Hearing and speaking though he was a house drawn
    Into silence, this was
        Something religious in his silence,

  Something shining in his quiet,
This was different this was altogether something else:
    Though he never spoke, this
        Was something to do with death.

  And then slowly the eye stopped looking
Inward. The silence rose and became still.
The look turned to the outer place and stopped,
    With the birds still shrilling around him.
      And as if he could speak

He turned over on his side with his one year
Red as a wound
He turned over as if he could be sorry for this
And out of his eyes two great tears rolled, like stones, and
      he died.

Jon Silkin

Beatrix Is Three

At the top of the stairs
I ask for her hand. O.K.
She gives it to me.
How her fist fits my palm,
A bunch of consolation.
We take our time
Down the steep carpetway
As I wish silently
That the stairs were endless.

Adrian Mitchell

To My Daughter

Bright clasp of her whole hand around my finger
My daughter, as we walk together now.
All my life I'll feel a ring invisibly
Circle this bone with shining; when she is grown
Far from today as her eyes are far already.

Stephen Spender

Jane at Play

I watch her in the garden and enjoy
Her serious enjoyment as she bends
And murmurs her grave nonsense to the toy
Circle of her animals and friends;
The doll that she quite obviously likes best
Would be to other eyes the ugliest.

For it is only later that we choose
To favour things which publish our good taste,
Whose beauty proves our talent to refuse
To dote upon the comic or defaced;
Unlike the child who needs no reference
Or cautious map to find her preference.

Yet we may be deceived by some old trick,
Robbed of our bright expensive instruments
And bundled from our path into the thick
Frondescence strangling all our arguments,
As when we see our child's plain loveliness
And blunder blind into our happiness.

Vernon Scannell

After Hugo

Jeanne Songeait ...

She was dreaming, sitting on the grass:
Her cheek was pink, her gaze was grave:
'Is there anything you would like to have?'
(I try to anticipate her least desire
To find what it is that sets her thoughts on fire.)
'Some animals,' she said — just that, no more:
I showed her an ant in the grass — 'There you are!'
But her imagination was left half-fed:
'No. Real animals are big,' she said.
Children dream of the vast, the ocean draws,
Cradles and calms them on the shore
With its rough music; its shadowiness
Will wholly captivate a child's mind,
And so will the terrifying flight of the sea-wind.
They love to be terrified, need wonder, feel no distress.
'I have no handy elephant,' I replied,
'So would you like something else — just say what.'
Pointing a small finger at the sky, she answered 'That!'
Evening would be overtaking the world soon —
I saw climbing up above the horizon an immense moon.

Charles Tomlinson

Tiger-taming

My small niece told me
that in his yellow toybox
the fierce tiger kept
a toy fierce tiger.

She had the same
yellow toybox.
The tiger's brilliance
roared out of it at her.

And the doll
she put to bed within —
one with her own blue eyes —
was twin for car journeys

and sitting up to eat her tea
or walks through the edges
of the nearby woods
where pigeons clattered suddenly.

She also told me
that when Goldilocks decided
she didn't want the porridge
and went next door instead,

the Three Bears rode away
on a red tricycle like hers.
We looked out of the window
and saw it parked by the gate.

Annemarie Austin

'Suddenly she is radiant again'

Suddenly she is radiant again.
She sees rainbows through her wet lashes;
In the brilliant light her wet cheeks glisten;
Her talk resumes like a brook, as fast and careless.

She has to suffer the interruption
Of sobs still, that have the bad manners
To arrive after the thunder has already gone
Over the hill, insisting they are hers.

We were a black sky only a minute ago,
Now I'm the one cloud in her clear heaven.
I haven't even begun yet to undo
The hideous knot of anger she tied me in.

I'm like a black old lump of winter snow
Bitterly facing the spring sun. Fair
Is always fair and the ugly, be they ever so
Much in the right, are not welcome anywhere.

I'm not a stone, I'm dirty snow that in
Her sunlight melts. It has no choice but to.
Soon I begin to feel I've been forgiven:
I go down on my knees and fasten her shoe.

David Constantine

Slow Reader

He can make sculptures
and fabulous machines,
invent games, tell jokes,
give solemn, adult advice —
but he is slow to read.
When I take him on my knee
with his Ladybird book
he gazes into the air,
sighing and shaking his head
like an old man
who knows the mountains
are impassable.

He toys with words,
letting them go cold
as gristly meat,
until I relent
and let him wriggle free:
a fish returning
to its element,
or a white-eyed colt — shying
from the bit — who sees
that if he takes it
in his mouth
he'll never run
quite free again.

Vicki Feaver

Walking Home (December 1948)

My hand in his and both inside his pocket.
Six years old and out at night, walking home.
Frost haloes ringed each street-lamp,
Round rainbows of yellow-green.
Cold air rasped my lungs.
Pavements glittered ice.

Our boots left hot black prints in white rime.
My toes would not separate.
The moon puffed cloud vapour across stars.
The world seemed bigger with its blue peeled back.
He'd told me once, 'Out there... that's Space.'
Rough tweed scratched my wrist.

His hand was very warm.
The smell of sawn logs seeped from his overalls.
'Look, there's The Plough,' he said,
'And there's The Giant.'
A giant farming the sky, I thought
And stared at the fields of space.

Catherine Benson

Two of Everything

My friend Shola said to me that she said to her mum:
'It's not fair, Carla (that's me) has two of everything:

Carla has two bedrooms,
two sets of toys, two telephones,

two wardrobes, two door mats
two mummies, two cats

two water purifiers, two kitchens,
two environmentally friendly squeezies.'

My friend Shola said to me that she said to her mum:
'Why can't you and Dad get divorced?'

But the thing Shola doesn't even realise yet,
is that there are two of me.

Jackie Kay

Catching Crabs

Ruby and me stalking savannah
Crab season with cutlass and sack like big folk.
Hiding behind stones or clumps of bush
Crabs locked knee-deep in mud mating
And Ruby seven years old feeling strange at the sex
And me horrified to pick them up
Plunge them into the darkness of bag,
So all day we scout to catch the lonesome ones
Who don't mind cooking because they got no prospect
Of family, and squelching through the mud,
Cutlass clearing bush at our feet,
We come home tired slow, weighed down with plenty
Which Ma throw live into boiling pot piece-piece.
Tonight we'll have one big happy curry feed.
We'll test out who teeth and jaw strongest
Who will grow up to be the biggest
Or who will make most terrible cannibal.

We leave behind a mess of bones and shell
And come to England and America
Where Ruby hustles in a New York tenement
And me writing poetry at Cambridge,
Death long catch Ma, the house boarded up
Breeding wasps, woodlice in its dark-sack belly:
I am afraid to walk through weed yard,
Reach the door, prise open, look,
In case the pot still bubbles magical
On the fireside, and I see Ma
Working a ladle, slow-
Limbed, crustacean-old, alone,
In case the woodsmoke and curry steam
Burn my child-eye and make it cry.

David Dabydeen

Broken Moon

for Emma

Twelve, small as six,
strength, movement, hearing
all given in half measure,
my daughter,
child of genetic carelessness,
walks uphill, always.

I watch her morning face;
precocious patience as she hooks each sock,
creeps it up her foot,
aims her jersey like a quoit.
My fingers twitch;
her private frown deters.

Her jokes can sting:
'My life is like dressed crab
— lot of effort, rather little meat.'
Yet she delights in seedlings taking root,
finding a fossil,
a surprise dessert.

Chopin will not yield to her stiff touch;
I hear her cursing.
She paces Bach exactly,
firm rounding of perfect cadences.
Somewhere inside
she is dancing a courante.

In dreams she skims the sand,
curls toes into the ooze of pools,
leaps on to stanchions.
Awake, her cousins take her hands;
they lean into the waves,
stick-child between curved sturdiness.

She turns away from stares,
laughs at the boy who asks
if she will find a midget husband.
Ten years ago, cradling her,
I showed her the slice of silver in the sky.
'Moon broken', she said.

Carole Satyamurti

Theresa

Theresa let fall her copy of *Harpers & Queen*
   and as it struck the ground (among her clothes,
books and several pairs of fat, unfashionable shoes) became a bird: her long nose longer, her slim
arms and fingers wings and golden feathers everywhere.

Her father was dismayed, her mother quite reluctant
   to remove the droppings from her cotton sheets.
They informed a priest: he took her silence to imply
   apostasy — a thoughtless rebellion.
She sat plump in the middle of the bed. Would not budge.

The trendy priest assumed a pose of concentration —
   skewering his clean-shaven chin with an oblong
index finger. Then he blessed her, then he left.
   Mother makes Theresa shallow bowls
of lemon tea. Bedside, Daddy delivers bulletins:

'I hang up when your spotty boyfriend telephones...'
   'Your mother is mixing gin and Librium...'
'I bought a new, smoke-blue Granada yesterday...'
   'Your mother insists on knowing when you fly...'
'The windows have been barred, we cannot let you fall...'

Stephen Knight

Waiting

The best place, when he is fractious,
is the British Museum, Egyptian Room.

There she sits on a bench
waiting for him, waiting for the time to pass.

She has waited for him in surgeries,
in special schools, in workshops;

waited for signs of improvement:
for the tide to turn.

Now he is peering at the embalmed animals
close-bandaged in their leak-marked linen.

He knocks on the glass with his knuckle,
at the skinny cat sitting up tall,

the baby-bull, the ducks and,
next to the crocodile, his own face

matching grin for grin. He raps harder
and she takes his arm.

Leave them alone. They won't wake up.
Hand in hand they walk away down the stairs

out past the pillars. She winds his scarf
tightly round him against the cold.

Connie Bensley

What Has Happened to Lulu?

What has happened to Lulu, mother?
  What has happened to Lu?
There's nothing in her bed but an old rag doll
  And by its side a shoe.

Why is her window wide, mother,
  The curtain flapping free,
And only a circle on the dusty shelf
  Where her money-box used to be?

Why do you turn your head, mother,
  And why do the tear-drops fall?
And why do you crumple that note on the fire
  And say it is nothing at all?

I woke to voices late last night,
  I heard an engine roar.
Why do you tell me the things I heard
  Were a dream and nothing more?

I heard somebody cry, mother,
  In anger or in pain,
But now I ask you why, mother,
  You say it was a gust of rain.

Why do you wander about as though
  You don't know what to do?
What has happened to Lulu, mother?
  What has happened to Lu?

Charles Causley

Outgrown

It is both sad and a relief to fold so carefully
her outgrown clothes and line up the little worn shoes
of childhood, so prudent, scuffed and particular.
It is both happy and horrible to send them galloping
back tappity-tap along the misty chill path into the past.

It is both a freedom and a prison, to be outgrown
by her as she towers over me as thin as a sequin
in her doc martens and her pretty skirt,
because just as I work out how to be a mother
she stops being a child.

Penelope Shuttle

Changes

My butterfly brooch is flitting off
Through the open window;
The hedgehog from the hearthstone moved
Sure though slow;
The bird in the picture on the tree
Has gone, and the real sea
Must have taken back the crabs and shells
We put in the pebble-filled watery jars.

Where, you ask, have our creatures gone?
They moved away when you left home.

Jenny Joseph

On a Son Returned to New Zealand

He is my green branch growing in a far plantation.
He is my first invention.

No one can be in two places at once.
So we left Athens on the same morning.
I was in a hot railway carriage, crammed
between Serbian soldiers and peasant
women, on sticky seats, with nothing to
drink but warm mineral water.
                                        He was
in a cabin with square windows, sailing
across the Mediterranean, fast,
to Suez.
            Then I was back in London
in the tarnished summer, remembering,
as I folded his bed up, and sent the
television set away. Letters came
from Aden and Singapore, late.
                                        He was
already in his father's house, on the
cliff-top, where the winter storms roll across
from Kapiti Island, and the flax bends
before the wind. He could go no further.

He is my bright sea-bird on a rocky beach.

Fleur Adcock

Walking Away

For Sean

It is eighteen years ago, almost to the day —
A sunny day with the leaves just turning,
The touch-lines new-ruled — since I watched you play
Your first game of football, then, like a satellite
Wrenched from its orbit, go drifting away

Behind a scatter of boys. I can see
You walking away from me towards the school
With the pathos of a half-fledged thing set free
Into a wilderness, the gait of one
Who finds no path where the path should be.

That hesitant figure, eddying away
Like a winged seed loosened from its parent stem,
Has something I never quite grasp to convey
About nature's give-and-take — the small, the scorching
Ordeals which fire one's irresolute clay.

I have had worse partings, but none that so
Gnaws at my mind still. Perhaps it is roughly
Saying what God alone could perfectly show —
How selfhood begins with a walking away,
And love is proved in the letting go.

Cecil Day Lewis

To a Son in the Middle East

Now that I know you're safe, anxiety
Casts with another fly. Now that you write
'Verandah', with a 'garden full of fruit',
I see a lizard humbly upside-down
Watching you read Herodotus; there's a fly
Slowly tacking towards the lizard's tongue.

And there's a charming rather sad young woman
Whose father is an officer who writes verse
In pencil on the back of battle-orders;
She hesitates by a fig-tree: is a fig
A proper gift to a foreigner in a room on
A hill? There's her timid, unfamiliar knock.

Is this the hill from which Tiglath-Pileser
Looked at the city on the eve of capture,
The kingdom Antony gave to Cleopatra
For a single kiss? If anything is given,
Make it the innocent kiss of sherbet: please her
With milk, snow, lemonade — as drunk in heaven.

Young women are always a bit imaginary;
But they're not treasure-trove. Their families
Still own them, watching there behind the trees
As the girl settles on your hand. Just try
To see her flight as they do: blow her free
Carefully as the angels flutter by.

Of course advice, the old man's voice, sounds shrill
To the young ear, and worse for being spelled
Out slowly. You would see the way I felt
Without such heavy words, if you were here:
Submissive to the inexperienced will
And interested in parental fear.

Alistair Elliot

' Go to your wide futures'

In Memory of my Mother

I do not think of you lying in the wet clay
Of a Monaghan graveyard; I see
You walking down a lane among the poplars
On your way to the station, or happily

Going to second Mass on a summer Sunday —
You meet me and you say:
'Don't forget to see about the cattle —'
Among your earthiest words the angels stray.

And I think of you walking along a headland
Of green oats in June,
So full of repose, so rich with life —
And I see us meeting at the end of a town

On a fair day by accident, after
The bargains are all made and we can walk
Together through the shops and stalls and markets
Free in the oriental streets of thought.

O you are not lying in the wet clay,
For it is a harvest evening now and we
Are piling up the ricks against the moonlight
And you smile up at us — eternally.

Patrick Kavanagh

At Ogmore-by-Sea This August Evening

I think of one who loved this estuary —
my father — who, self-taught, scraped upon
an obstinate violin. Now, in a room
darker than the darkening evening outside,
I choose a solemn record, listen to
a violinist inhabit a Bach partita.
This violinist and violin are unified.

Such power! The music summons night. What more?
It's twenty minutes later into August
before the gaudy sun sinks to Australia.
Now nearer than the promontory paw
and wincing electric of Porthcawl
look! the death-boat black as anthracite,
at its spotlit prow a pale familiar.

Father? Here I am, Father. I see you
jubilantly lit, an ordered carnival.
The tide's in. From Nash Point no foghorns howl.
I'm at your favourite place where once you held
a bending rod and taught me how to bait
the ragworm hooks. Here, Father, here, tonight
we'll catch a bass or two, or dabs, or cod.

Senseless conjuration! I wipe my smile away
for now, lit at the prow, not my father
but his skeleton stands. The spotlight fails,
the occult boat's a smudge while three far lighthouses
converse in dotty exclamation marks.
The ciaccona's over, the record played,
there's nothing but the tumult of the sea.

Dannie Abse

Praise Song for My Mother

You were
water to me
deep and bold and fathoming

You were
moon's eye to me
pull and grained and mantling

You were
sunrise to me
rise and warm and streaming

You were
the fishes red gill to me
the flame tree's spread to me
the crab's leg/the fried plantain smell
            replenishing replenishing

Go to your wide futures, you said

Grace Nichols

Lineage

When my eyes were sore or tired or itched,
clenching her hand in a loose fist,
my mother would rub her wedding ring,
carefully, along the closed lids,
sure the touch of gold was curative.

She also believed in hot water
with lemon, first thing in the morning
and, at any time of day, drank awful-
tasting infusions and pot-liquors
to purify her blood. She warmed
a spoonful of sweet almond oil to pour
into my aching ear, wrapped torn
old woollen vests around my throat,
and blistered my chest with a poultice
if I came down with a cold.

Remedies and simples from the old
country, still useful in the city,
were passed from mother to daughter
and not yet scorned. We rarely saw
a doctor. When I was little
it seemed normal to be sickly
for half of the year. I never told her
that I was proud she was a witch.

Ruth Fainlight

After Mammy Telt Me She Wisnae My Real Mammy

After mammy telt me she wisnae my real mammy
I was scared to death she was gonnie melt
or something or mibbe disappear in the dead
of night and somebody would say she wis a fairy
godmother. So the next morning I felt her skin
to check it was flesh, but mibbe it was just
a good imitation. How could I tell if my mammy
was a dummy with a voice spoken by someone else?
So I searches the whole house for clues
but I never found nothing. Anyhow a day after
I got my guinea pig and forgot all about it.

Jackie Kay

Looking for Dad

Whenever Mum and Dad
were full of gloom
they always yelled
'Tidy up your room!'
Just because my comics were
scattered here and
everywhere and
because I did not care
where I left my underwear
they yelled, *'You can't watch tv today*
unless you clear that terrible mess away!'
Then one day they
could not care less
about my room's
awful mess.
They seemed more intent
on having what they called
a domestic argument.
They both looked glum
and instead of at me Dad
screeched at Mum.
One night when I
went to bed he
simply vanished.
I had not tidied
up my room because I too
was full of gloom.
That night I dreamt
Dad was hidden
beneath the things
I'd been given.
In my dream
I was in despair
and flung around
my underwear
but could not find
Dad anywhere.

I looked for him
lots and lots
beneath crumpled sheets
and old robots.
In my dream
I looked in cupboards
and in shoes,
I looked up all
the chimney flues.
I remembered how
he seemed to be
unhappier than
even me.
When I woke I knew
it was not my room
that filled Mum and Dad
with so much gloom.
Now I stare at all
my old toy cars
and carpets stained
with old Mars bars
and hope he will
come back soon
and admire my very
tidy room.

Brian Patten

My Papa's Waltz

The whiskey on your breath
Could make a small boy dizzy;
But I hung on like death:
Such waltzing was not easy.

We romped until the pans
Slid from the kitchen shelf;
My mother's countenance
Could not unfrown itself.

The hand that held my wrist
Was battered on one knuckle;
At every step you missed
My right ear scraped a buckle.

You beat time on my head
With a palm caked hard by dirt,
Then waltzed me off to bed
Still clinging to your shirt.

Theodore Roethke

Stellar Manipulator

I

Judge Durcan, you wanted
Your eldest son to be a lawyer.
But wanting always to be
Like the other you, Daddy,
To become your understudy,
I became at the age of twenty-five
Stellar Manipulator
At the London Planetarium.

When I went for the interview
With the Director of the Planetarium,
John Ebdon,
He so much looked
And sounded like you
I had to be careful not
To address him as Daddy.
'I hear that you write
Poetry' — he exclaimed.
I winced. He continued:
Many a night I saw the Pleiads,
rising through the mellow shade,
Glitter like a swarm of fire-flies
tangled in a silver braid.
When I failed to identify
The author, he said
'Tennyson' — and gave me the job.

II

Seven a.m. on a black Sunday morning
In Ladbroke Grove.
The black telephone. Your black voice.
'This is Harrow Road Police Station:
You are requested to act as bailsman.'
Down at the station at 7.45 a.m.
The duty officer takes down details.
Status: Married. *Sex:* Male.

Nationality: Irish. *Age:* 25.
Occupation: Stellar Manipulator.
The duty officer focuses his eyes
And asks me to repeat my occupation
That he can note it down correctly.
I say it with deliberation,
pronouncing solemnly each syllable:
'Stell-ar Man-ip-ul-at-or.'
He smiles as you used to smile, Daddy,
If ever there was so much as the remotest
Rumour of humour in the universe,
A smidgen of light in the black.

III

Back home in Dublin
In the locker room of the golf club,
When other members of the fourball
Enquire after your eldest son,
Knowing that I am the black
Sheep of the family,
Thinking to get a rise out of you,
'Well, what's he working at now?'
You take your time,
Scrutinising the clay adhering
To the studs of your golf shoes,
Scraping it off with a penknife.
Your rejoinder is indifferent,
Laconic, offhand:
'He's a —' satisfactorily
Flaking off another lump of clay,
'Stellar Manipulator.'

Paul Durcan

The Way My Mother Speaks

I say her phrases to myself
in my head
or under the shallows of my breath,
restful shapes moving.
The day and ever. The day and ever.

The train this slow evening
goes down England
browsing for the right sky,
too blue swapped for a cool grey.
For miles I have been saying
What like is it
the way I say things when I think.
Nothing is silent. Nothing is not silent.
What like is it.

Only tonight
I am happy and sad
like a child
who stood at the end of summer
and dipped a net
in a green, erotic pond. *The day*
and ever. The day and ever.
I am homesick, free, in love
with the way my mother speaks.

Carol Ann Duffy

Vacation Jobs

Two summers a shipwrights' labourer
my Old Man wangled, of me humping
toolbags, timber, learning to batten
hatches, torn-off cars down holds;
then a single summer in the General Stores
among old men like budgies chunnering
in dingy corners of quayside sheds...

same Company he was foreman rigger for,
same grey gull-infested wharves
and yellow-funnel boats that slogged
the South America run: his world
and workplace where he knew respect...

ask anyone, Old Lars, Pongo, Billy Molloy,
ask any skipper, engineer, or mate along
the line of docks: always a good word,
a tot or two, a backhander bottle of
Bacardi rum for him...

who bungled things back home,
across the nervous tablecloth or in
the blue flicker of telly or loud behind
bedroom doors: he wanted me to witness
the respect he walked about in there,
along wharves, over decks, in messrooms,
to know what I was forfeiting, know it for real.

Matt Simpson

Now That I Hear Trains

Now that I hear trains
whistling out of Paddington on their way to Wales,
I like to think of him, as young as he was then,
running behind me along the sand,
holding my saddle steady
and launching me off on my own.

Now that I look unlike
the boy on the brand new bike
who wobbled away down the beach,
I hear him telling me: 'Keep pedalling, keep pedalling.'
When I looked over my shoulder
he was nowhere to be seen.

Hugo Williams

Mother Stone

My father was a tall man who approved of beating,
but my mother, like a mother stone,
preferred us to be sitting in a small room
lined with damson-coloured velvet
thinking quietly to ourselves, undisturbed;
everything was slow and beautiful
when we were being punished: all we had to do
was watch the dark-red petals' roses
press against each other in a slight breeze
on the window pane, and blossoms fall
in silence from the cherry tree;

and now my son is lying in a long white shirt
across our eiderdown, trying to stay awake,
and fingering my spine's shell pink as if I were a beach
and he were blades of marram grass in drifts of sand.
I dab my face with cream that smells of cucumber
and whisper in a distant milky voice
Of course I'll wake you up when he comes;
and then his eyelids close,
and in his self-created darkness he is following
a big car on a motorway at night,
it turns into the driveway to the house,
and presently the driver gets out:
it is only a bear in the moonlight,
walking on the lavender beds.

Selima Hill

Memory of My Father

Every old man I see
Reminds my of my father
When he had fallen in love with death
One time when sheaves were gathered.

That man I saw in Gardner Street
Stumble on the kerb was one,
He stared at me half-eyed,
I might have been his son.

And I remember the musician
Faltering over his fiddle
In Bayswater, London,
He too set me the riddle.

Every old man I see
In October-coloured weather
Seems to say to me:
'I was once your father'.

Patrick Kavanagh

Mansize

Now you aren't here I find
myself ironing linen squares,
three by three, the way
my mother's always done,
the steel tip steaming over your
blue initial. I, who resent
the very thought of this back-breaking
ritual, preferring radiator-dried
cottons, stiff as boards, any amount
of crease and crumple to this
soothing, time-snatching, chore.

I never understood my father's trick,
his spare for emergencies, but was glad
of its airing-cupboard comforts often enough:
burying my nose in it, drying my eyes
with it, staunching my blood with it,
stuffing my mouth with it. His expedience,
my mother's weekly art, leaves me
forever flawed: rushing into newsagents
for Kleenex, rifling your pockets in the cinema,
falling on those cheap printed florals,

when what I really want is Irish linen,
shaken out for me to sink my face in,
the shape and scent of you still warm
in it, your monogram in chainstitch
at the corner. Comforter, seducer, key witness
to it all, my neatly folded talisman,
my sweet flag of surrender.

Maura Dooley

When the camel is dust
it goes through the needle's eye

This hot summer wind
is tiring my mother.
It tires her to watch it
buffeting the poppies.
Down they bow
in their fluttering kimonos,
a suppressed populace,
an unpredictable dictator.

The silver-haired reeds
are also supplicants.
Stripped of its petals,
clematis looks grey
on the wall. My mother,
who never came here,
suggests it's too hot
to cook supper.

Her tiredness gets everywhere
like blown topsoil,
teasing my eyes and tongue,
wrinkling my skin.
Summer after summer, silt
becomes landfill between us,
level and walkable,
level, eventually, and simple.

Anne Stevenson

Virtuoso

Before you could say knife
I can slit his pile of letters
almost to ribbons, slide the paper streamers
into his hands. You should see me
fly upstairs to fetch glasses,
pencil, slippers — collapse
a wheelchair with one finger, raise his zimmer
high in the dazed lamp-light
and twirl it. I can
slip through a door backwards,
forwards, sideways, with or without
spare trousers. I can balance
his full tea-cup on one knee and never
spill a drop, as love
mashes to leaves.
                        If you could
call him just once, if you could let me
hear the true cadence
of *darling, sweetheart, my dearest,* I would even
comfort him. I would practise and practise.

Susan Wicks

First Day of Spring

A good day to plant you in good earth, dad,
as you seemed to tell us (as a gardener should).
The sun came with the flowers. You should have seen
the wide sweep of the view across to Mawstone
from your plot. 'Grand,' you would have called it.
I had this mad idea of sowing lilac-seeds
inside the grave because you told us once,
when we were planting shoots too near the house,
that when the roots spread they would crack foundations.
I suppose they would have been too deep to sprout.
In any case, the vicar said I mustn't
but I needed your professional advice.
We buried you in polished elm. For preference
I would have chosen ash — not just
because of your redundant walking-stick;
I was thinking of the whistles you used to make for us,
whittling at the wood with your pocket-knife,
keeping the smooth sheath of the bark intact.
'My turn next!' we clamoured as we followed
in your footsteps up Spring Lane as if
you were the Pied Piper. (Funny thing to think about,
following your bier out of the shade into bright sunlight.)
Anyway, you timed it right. I don't know what
you would have thought about the forced tulips
but the daffodils ought to have been seasonable.
Everything was late this year, up north,
and there was still snow where the sun didn't reach.
I must say this, though, right away, before I forget:
back home I spent hours studying your crocuses —
smaller than last year, but somehow ceremonious —
gold, royal blue, a nameless shade of white.

Sylvia Kantaris

'Close-dancing families'

To My Brothers

Small, busy flames play through the fresh laid coals,
    And their faint cracklings o'er our silence creep
    Like whispers of the household gods that keep
A gentle empire o'er fraternal souls.
And while, for rhymes, I search around the poles,
    Your eyes are fix'd, as in poetic sleep,
    Upon the lore so voluble and deep,
That aye at fall of night our care condoles.
This is your birth-day Tom, and I rejoice
    That thus it passes smoothly, quietly.
Many such eves of gently whisp'ring noise
    May we together pass, and calmly try
What are this world's true joys,—ere the great voice,
    From its fair face, shall bid our spirits fly.

John Keats

For a Family Album

Four heads in one lamp's light
And each head bowed into peculiar darkness,
Reading, drawing, alone.
A camera would have caught them, held them there
Half-lit in the room's warm halflight,
Left them, refused to tell
How long till that lamp was broken,
Your hair pinned up or cut or tinted or waved.

I cannot even describe them, caught no more
Than a flash of light that ripped open
The walls of our half-lit room;
Or the negative — a black wedge
Rammed into light so white that it hurt to look.

Leave this page blank.
You'd neither like nor believe
The picture no lens could have taken:

Tied to my rooted bones
In your chairs you were flying, flying.

Michael Hamburger

A634 NKX

When the old ambulance broke down
my sister's kids got out and pushed,
all nine of them, and gradually
she'd be driving towards another birth,
picking up indecent speed, laughing
like the two-year-old in the wake
of the suddenly farted-out smoke.
She'd thank God as the engine coughed
and there was life, as a heave of labours
grew in the mirror into a stampede of souls,
more laughter in the English suburbs.

Lance, they called it, for short.
It smothered Father Patrick's weekends,
clipped the kerbs of dreams at night
when faded into abortive silence,
collected stray leaves between tyres,

while under their posters of turtles, cars
and the Blessed Virgin Mary, they slept
on the smooth rides of their bunk-beds,
my sister and her nine loves,
freewheeling towards another green light.

Paul Henry

Windy's House

(For my sisters)

Smell of banana bread warming itself to golden brown
moist inside, walnuts, the ones baby Sally always picks out.
Old wood and eucalyptus, steady thud of grandfather's clock
the lazy pendulum. Coffee on the drip. A sea of calm drifts
    through you
the quiet that comes when you know you're home,
safe place where you can be or not be
as still as that squirrel on the branch of the mossy oak.
The piano plays ragtime in another room, switches to a lullaby
shushing the bad dreams back into the cotton-sweet closet.
You know where you are in the soft bed,
the same painting, same photographs
all your life, all their voices.
You will not want to leave this place ever,
a sister's love will wrap such strong arms around you,
murmur, *it's okay, it's all right* and for a flash of a moment
you believe her, your life depends on it.

Judi Benson

Chicken Poxed

My sister was spotty, real spotty all over,
She was plastered with spots from her head to her toes,
She had spots on the parts that the bathing suits cover,
Spots on her eyelids and spots on her nose.

I didn't know chicken pox was so interesting,
It seemed a great shame to waste all those spots,
So when Jody was sleeping and no-one was looking,
I got a blue pen and connected her dots.

Valerie Bloom

The Baby of the Family

Up on Daddy's shoulders
He is riding high —
The baby of the family,
A pleased pork pie.
I'm tired and my feet are sore —
It seems all wrong.
He's lucky to be little
But it won't last long.

The baby of the family,
He grabs my toys
And when I grab them back he makes
A big, loud noise.
I mustn't hit him, so I chant
This short, sweet song:
'You're lucky to be little
But it won't last long.'

Everybody looks at him
And thinks he's sweet,
Even when he bellows 'No!'
And stamps his feet.
He won't be so amusing
When he's tall and strong.
It's lovely being little
But it won't last long.

Wendy Cope

Poem For My Sister

My little sister likes to try my shoes,
to strut in them,
admire her spindle-thin twelve-year-old legs
in this season's styles.
She says they fit her perfectly,
but wobbles
on their high heels, they're
hard to balance.

I like to watch my little sister
playing hopscotch, admire the neat hops-and-skips of her,
their quick peck,
never-missing their mark, not
over-stepping the line.
She is competent at peever.

I try to warn my little sister
about unsuitable shoes,
point out my own distorted feet, the callouses,
odd patches of hard skin.
I should not like to see her
in my shoes.
I wish she would stay
sure footed,
        sensibly shod.

Liz Lochhead

Sisters

My sister
was the bad one —
said what she thought
and did what she liked
and didn't care.

At ten she wore
a knife tucked in
her leather belt,
dreamed of *being*
a prince on a white horse.

Became a dolly bird
with dyed hair longer
than her skirts, pulling˙
the best of the local talent.
Mother wept and prayed.

At thirty she's divorced,
has cropped her locks
and squats in Hackney —
tells me, 'God created man
then realised her mistake.'

I'm not like her,
I'm good — but now
I'm working on it.
Fighting through
to my own brand of badness

I am glad of her
at last — her conferences,
her anger, and her boots.
We talk and smoke
and laugh at everybody —

two bad sisters.

Wendy Cope

Memorial

David Redgrove: 28 December 1937—24 December 1957

Two photographs stand on the dresser
Joined up the spine. Put away
They fold until they kiss each other,
But put out, they look across the room.
My brother and myself. He is flushed and pouting
With heart, and standing square,
I, already white-browed and balding,
Float there, it seems, and look away.
You could look at us and say I was the one of air,
And he the brother of earth
Who, in Christmas-time, fell to his death.

Fancy, yes; but if you'd seen him in his life
There'd be his bright blond hair, and that flush,
And the mouth always slightly open, and the strength
Of body: those muscles! swelled up with the hard
                                        hand-springs at night
Certainly, but strong. I, on the other hand
Was remote, cross, and disengaged, a proper
Bastard to my brother, who enjoyed things,
Until he was able to defend himself. It's June;
Everything's come out in flush and white,
In ruff and sun, and tall green shoots
Hard with their sap. He's ashes
Like this cigarette I smoke into grey dryness.
I notice outside my window a tree of blossom,
Cherries, I think, one branch bending heavy
Into the grey road to its no advantage.
The hard stone scrapes the petals off,
And the dust enters the flower into its peak.

Peter Redgrove

Siblings United

For Eithne at 21

Not a care tonight
about which of the family
is out late, sharing the roads
with reckless drivers
or who is short of money,
feeling out of sorts.
We are all here, survivors,
converging at your twenty-first.
You are no longer a child
and I am no longer required
to act as trustee
of our father's will.

United, we declare your independence.
I drink to your health
along with workmates
(you have a full-time job now,
plan a fortnight in France)
or I chat to a slim cousin
remembered with fat legs
propelling a toy scooter,
uncles last seen at a funeral.
We pose for photographs,
slip arms round waists
like life belts...

You cut through your name,
dripped in sugar icing
on the home-made cake,
expose the darker
layers underneath.
A close-dancing family
tonight, we celebrate

that you have come of age:
affable, happy, relaxed
in your floral party dress,
showing no after-effects
of your years of grief.

Dennis O'Driscoll

Siblings Revisited

Declan at Twenty

Only a few years ago, it was Jennings schoolboy stories
that I brought you. Now, I pack avant-garde books:
Tom Mallin, Alan Burns, a B.S. Johnson play.

'There isn't enough enthusiasm in the world', you always
    tell me.
And yours is revealed, petitioning for the release of prisoners,
contributing a series entitled 'Freedom' to *The Tipperary Star,*
reading African novelists, surveying a heron's nest,
displaying your unframed paintings along the bedroom wall.
In one corner, where a cliff of rock magazines used to rise,
back issues of *New Statesman* pile — the town's sole subscriber.
Of late, you have taken to playing the trumpet,
scorning sheet music in favour of the improvised tune.

You were maturing, swelling with cells, as parental death loomed,
called twice from the classroom for grim news.
I hint at the advantages of further studies sometimes.
Without success. And out of your seasonal job, of bog work,
you pay for essentials: subscriptions, membership fees, jazz LPs.
On blustery days, I wonder if the wind is with or against you
as you cycle there, along unsheltered miles ...
Play me, improvise on the trumpet, the rhythm of your new life.
Blast me the notes of your freedom.
Show me how to extend past experience to joy.

Dennis O'Driscoll

Nant Gwrtheyrn

Clouds accumulate, darkening
The worn face of the mountain. The striped
Cry of the oyster-catcher cuts
The sky. Impossible to join the spaces.

One mass against another. Frail
Sounds falling like ribbons or wounds.
Bits creeping, vegetation,
Distraction under the small rain.

The sisters clump up the Nant in boots,
Damp hair close to the forehead, sorrel
In warm folds of the palm, feathers
And granite sugar, so far ahead.

One lingers on the path, smooth grass
Where sheep have nibbled. The blue husk
Of a tiger beetle cradled there
Is spiritless, an Egyptian relic.

It is borne up the valley, joining
One thing with another. The day
Lightens. Clouds break up the sky.
Jerseys are tied around the waist.

The spaces grow between them, dislinked
On the gradient, frowning and looking
Back. The battered sky opens.
The treasures slip from opening fingers.

John Fuller

My Aunts

My aunts jived their way
Through the Fifties to my teens.
They lay till noon and called me up
To listen for their lovers at the gate,
And paid me for the colour of their eyes —
'Grey', I said, or 'Brown', when they wanted
Blue or hazel, in their giggling,
Sleeping-together dreams.

I watched them shading in their lips
From sugar pink to coral, from mulberry to rose,
And their wet skirts hungry for
The brilliance of their swing,
As they dried by the strange
Elastic girdles, paper petticoats.

Once out of the blue
I caught them dancing on the bed,
With their undergrowth of hazel,
And their make-up sweated through.

Medbh McGuckian

Guidance

Wash yuh han dem before yuh eat
Sit still, stop twitching in yuh seat,
Don' bang the plate with yuh knife an' fork,
An' keep quiet when big people a-talk
Stop drag yuh foot dem pon the floor,
Ah tell yuh a'ready, don' slam the door,
Cover up yuh mout when you a cough,
Don' be greedy, give yuh sister half
O' the banana that yuh eating there,
What kind o' dress that yuh a-wear?
Don' hiss yuh teeth when me talk to yuh,
And mind how yuh looking at me too,
Teck me good advice, me girl,
Manners carry yuh through the worl',
Ah tellin yuh this fe yuh own good
Yuh should thank me, show some gratitude,

Life is really tough for me,
When Uncle Henry comes to tea.

Valerie Bloom

Aunt Julia

Aunt Julia spoke Gaelic
very loud and very fast.
I could not answer her —
I could not understand her.

She wore men's boots
when she wore any.
— I can see her strong foot,
stained with peat,
paddling the treadle of the spinning wheel
while her right hand drew yarn
marvellously out of the air.

Hers was the only house
where I lay at night
in the absolute darkness
of the box bed, listening to
crickets being friendly.

She was buckets
and water flouncing into them.
She was winds pouring wetly
round house-ends.
She was brown eggs, black skirts
and a keeper of threepennybits
in a teapot.

Aunt Julia spoke Gaelic
very loud and very fast.
By the time I had learned
a little, she lay
silenced in the absolute black
of a sandy grave
at Luskentyre.
But I hear her still, welcoming me
with a seagull's voice
across a hundred yards

of peatscapes and lazybeds
and getting angry, getting angry
with so many questions
unanswered.

Norman MacCaig

Sad Aunt Madge

As the cold winter evenings drew near
Aunt Madge used to put extra blankets
over the furniture, to keep it warm and cosy
Mussolini was her lover, and life
was an outoffocus rosy tinted spectacle,

but neurological experts
with kind blueeyes
and gentle voices
small white hands
and large Rolls Royces
said that electric shock treatment
should do the trick
it did ...

today after 15 years of therapeutic tears
and an awful lot of ratepayers' shillings
down the hospital meter
sad Aunt Madge
no longer tucks up the furniture
before kissing it goodnight
and admits
that her affair with Mussolini
clearly was not right
particularly in the light
of her recently announced engagement
to the late pope.

Roger McGough

Granny on Her Singer Sewing Machine

You think you are a bird and your station is the sky?
Lick the thread and feed it through the needle's eye.

Are you an eagle or a hawk prepared to kill and die?
Lick the thread and feed it through the needle's eye.

When the enemy clips your wings explain how you'll fly?
Lick the thread and feed it through the needle's eye.

You hardly smell your sweat, don't fall for the old lie;
Lick the thread and feed it through the needle's eye.

Fred D'Aguiar

A House of Mercy

It was a house of female habitation,
Two ladies fair inhabited the house,
And they were brave. For although Fear knocked loud
Upon the door, and said he must come in,
They did not let him in.

There were also two feeble babes, two girls,
That Mrs S. had by her husband had,
He soon left them and went away to sea,
Nor sent them money, nor came home again
Except to borrow back
Her Naval Officer's Wife's Allowance from Mrs S.
Who gave it him at once, she thought she should.

There was also the ladies' aunt
And babes' great aunt, a Mrs Martha Hearn Clode,
And she was elderly.
These ladies put their money all together
And so we lived.

I was the younger of the feeble babes
And when I was a child my mother died
And later Great Aunt Martha Hearn Clode died
And later still my sister went away.

Now I am old I tend my mother's sister
The noble aunt who so long tended us,
Faithful and True her name is. Tranquil.
Also Sardonic. And I tend the house.

It is a house of female habitation
A house expecting strength as it is strong
A house of aristocratic mould that looks apart
When tears fall; counts despair
Derisory. Yet it has kept us well. For all its faults,
If they are faults, of sternness and reserve,
It is a Being of warmth I think; at heart
A house of mercy.

Stevie Smith

For My Grandmother

Aaji, there was an eleven-year-old girl
who sat on our doorstep
during the feast
of your mourning.
She would not cry or eat
                    sleep or speak.
Now they make dolls
who do all of those things.

            And I could not explain
            about my taut
            four hours of sleep
            in the closet, on the floor
            with your softly dying clothes.

Sujata Bhatt

108

Jack

She tells her grandchildren how her brother went
Off in the ambulance, his big laced boots
Heavy on the stretcher at the ends of legs
So white and thin. A family event,
The prelude to a funeral. She puts
A storyteller's shape on what she says,
And what she says holds them and makes them see
That Yorkshire street, those other, different days.

At nine years old her brother went, when we
Were nowhere, her grandchildren further off
Even than that. An accident, a death.

She pauses suddenly. The unwilled tears come,
She drops her face, and with a little cough
Stops the recital. Round the shadowy room
Children and grandchildren are silent too,
Life standing like a weight we cannot move,
Unmuscled by the thin, sharp shaft of love
That still must wound, and still the wound must show

And all that happened sixty years ago.

Anthony Thwaite

Granny Granny Please Comb my Hair

Granny Granny please comb
my hair
you always take your time
you always take such care

You put me on a cushion
between your knees
you rub a little coconut oil
parting gentle as a breeze

Mummy Mummy
she's always in a hurry-hurry
rush
she pulls my hair
sometimes she tugs

But Granny
you have all the time
in the world
and when you're finished
you always turn my head and say
'Now who's a nice girl'

Grace Nichols

Granny

Granny is
fried dumplin' an' run-rung,
coconut drops an' grater cake,
fresh-ground coffee smell in the mornin'
when we wake.

Granny is
loadin' up the donkey
basket full up on market day
with fresh snapper the fishermen bring back
from the bay.

Granny is
clothes washin' in the river
scrubbin' dirt out on the stone
haulin' crayfish an' eel from water
on her own.

Granny is
stories in the moonlight
underneath the guango tree
and a spiderweb of magic
all round we.

Granny say
all the best for the gran'children
it no matter what the price
don't want no-one pointin' finger.

Granny nice.

Valerie Bloom

My Grandmother

We all called her Gong-Gong.
Nothing to do with dinner bells.
Nothing to do with Buddhism.

I used to slip-slide my arm
up her narrow nightgown sleeve,
so I'd know when she wriggled,

salmon-like, to get out of bed.
They found us plaited that way
when she simply ups and died.

The unravelling took my mother
several long minutes on end;
I refused to let my Gong-Gong

go away, easy, just like that,
all on her own, into the night
of moonlight and splashy shadows.

Andrew Salkey

Grandad

Grandad's dead
And I'm sorry about that.

He'd a huge black overcoat.
He felt proud in it.
You could have hidden
A football crowd in it.
Far too big—
It was a lousy fit
But Grandad didn't
Mind a bit.
He wore it all winter
With a squashed black hat.

Now he's dead
And I'm sorry about that.

He'd got twelve stories.
I'd heard every one of them
Hundreds of times
But that was the fun of them:
You knew what was coming
So you could join in.
He'd got big hands
And brown, grooved skin
And when he laughed
It knocked you flat.

Now he's dead
And I'm sorry about that.

Kit Wright

Grandparents

They stand at the door
Like figures in a weather house,
Waving to their children's cars.

If he goes first she'll protest
Against help, hating the need,
Lost among his unused things,
Forgetting to bake for visitors.
Suds will never loosen her rings.

And if she goes he'll proclaim
Independence, strictly his own man,
Yet attend to room with her methods.
On Sundays he'll snooze among grandchildren,
Telling worn jokes, afraid to spill soup.

Sean Dunne

First Meeting with
a Possible Mother-in-Law

She thought, without the benefit of knowing,
You, who had been hers, were not any more.
We had locked our love in to leave nothing showing
From the room her handiwork had crammed before;
But — much revealing in its figured sewing —
A piece of stuff hung out, caught in the door.
I caused the same suspicion I watched growing:
Who could not tell what whole the part stood for?

There was small likeness between her and me:
Two strangers left upon a bare top landing,
I for a prudent while, she totally.

But, eyes turned from the bright material hint,
Each shared too long a second's understanding,
Learning the other's terms of banishment.

Thom Gunn

Dumb Show

Freesias are such badly orchestrated flowers,
Dear mother-in-law, whom I may not call
Mother-in-law. The flowers succeed each other,
And when the first limp head spells death
I want to compost the lot. You innocently say
There's so much still to come. There is.
I prise from their green sockets
The moribund daily, severely. How should you know
What it is I remember, who gave me these flowers
When she went away, and I, to keep her close,
Endlessly doctored stalks? Fit emblem of a friendship
I wanted to be love, and made drag on
Until its florist's gleam was mildewed, rotten.

                                    At ninety-two,
You have your reasons too for keeping flowers
Beyond their common span.

U.A. Fanthorpe

116

Shawl

Mamgu, a century old, loops coloured wool.
She can't see them now. The shawl

is in her mind. She touches colour.
Her fingers fly as bats at dusk in summer,

bringing the dark. The shawl grows over her knees
heavy as shadows lengthening under trees.

Her fingers write on air. She talks, walking
the old roads, tarmac'ed now, but in her mind

bone-white, scuffed by the boots of girls trailing
their hems in dust. She takes each bend,

each hill, gives every field its name.
Her hands cross-hatch the air. Garden and room

are gradually shadowed, her psalms'
memorial litany, a list of farms.

Gillian Clarke
Note: Mamgu = grandmother in Welsh

An Addition to the Family

for M.L.

A musical poet, collector of basset-horns,
was buttering his toast down in Dunbartonshire
when suddenly from behind the breakfast newspaper
the shining blade stopped scraping
and he cried to his wife, 'Joyce, listen to this! —
"Two basset-hounds for sale, house-trained, keen hunters" —
Oh we must have them! What d'you think?' 'But dear,
did you say hounds?' 'Yes yes, hounds, hounds —'
'But Maurice, it's horns we want, you must be over
in the livestock column, what would we do
with a basset-hound, you can't play a hound!'
'It's Beverley it says, the kennels are at Beverley —'
'But Maurice —' '— I'll get some petrol, we'll be there
        by lunchtime —'
'But a dog, two dogs, where'll we put them?'
'I've often wondered what these dogs are like —'
'You mean you don't even —' 'Is there no more marmalade?'
'— don't know what they look like? And how are we to
        feed them?
Yes, there's the pot dear.' 'This stuff's all peel, isn't it?'
'Well, we're at the end of it. But look, these two great —'
'You used to make marmalade once upon a time.'
'They've got ears down to here, and they're far too —'
'Is that half past eight? I'll get the car out.
See if I left my cheque-book on the —' 'Maurice,
are you mad? What about your horns?' 'What horns,
what are you talking about? Look Joyce dear,
if it's not on the dresser it's in my other jacket.
I believe they're wonderful for rabbits —'
So the musical poet took his car to Beverley
with his wife and his cheque-book, and came back home
with his wife and his cheque-book and two new hostages
to the unexpectedness of fortune.

The creatures scampered through the grass, the children
came out with cries of joy, there seemed to be nothing
dead or dying in all that landscape.
Fortune bless the unexpected cries!
Life gathers to the point of wishing it,
a mocking pearl of many ventures. The house
rolled on its back and kicked its legs in the air.
And later, wondering farmers as they passed would hear
behind the lighted window in the autumn evening
two handsome mellow-bosomed basset-hounds
howling to a melodious basset-horn.

Edwin Morgan

Family

When you swim in the surf off Seal Rocks, and your family
Sits in the sand
Eating potato salad, and the undertow
Comes which takes you out away down
To loss of breath loss of play and the power of play
Holler, say
Help, help, help. Hello, they will say,
Come back here for some potato salad.

It is then that a seventeen-year-old cub
Cruising in a helicopter from Antigua,
A jackstraw expert speaking only Swedish
And remote from this area as a camel, says
Look down there, there is somebody drowning.

And it is you. You say, yes, yes,
And he throws you a line.
This is what is called the brotherhood of man.

Josephine Miles

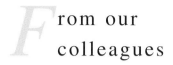

Family

Of course there were uncles. They would come in
and often go out again. Did men
really live in one place? Would they rather be gone
that let places, table and lamp tie them down?

"Dear me, such ants in his pants." Not Granddad, though.
His wicker chair beside the moss-covered bowl
with goldfish. He had an easy way
of telling sons and hired hands what to do.

Sensitive plant grew in the greenhouse.
"If you touch it too much it gets tired."
Just one more time frightened green. The question why
they raised it was not for children to ask.

The farmhouse kitchen is loud with flies. Black
the enormous stove. Grandmother sits
at the table with the cashbox. As if she's not
been his wife for ages, she's matter-of-fact

when you want to know something: "Now that
I don't know, child. Just ask De Wit."

Willem van Toorn (The Netherlands)
Translation Myra Scholz

West Flanders

its water that hardly flows to the sea,
its sand, its polders and all its farmlands,
its discos, casinos and pastry shops,
its folk-rooted wisdom, its side-splitting jokes:
the landscape lies open like a diary
but is readable only as braille.

with its gut-level balking at progress or change,
it's a land of tamed passions, well-behaved fun
always carefully budgeted in,
money they count there like rosary beads.

some Fridays there's a smell of soapsuds and brine,
when the women, in a heat for having things clean,
scrub away at front steps and front walks.
their husbands, delighted to see them work hard,
will drag them out later for a day at the sea.

grief does not exist here, no one wastes time
on a pastime so pointless.
for sadness there is the lavatory
where you can break wind and break down,
heave sigh upon sob and flush them away,
gathering solace for the living room.

but one Sunday evening in August,
with lemonade and raspberry ice-cream,
I heard my mother singing here.
the air was dizzy with dahlias and roses,
a late blackbird was still skimming past.
she sang, and this scene stayed with me so long
that when she died and was buried here
it turned a little less cold in this ground.

Luuc Gruwez (Belgium)
Translation Myra Scholz

*I*ndex

• Irish poets and poets selected by
people living in the Republic of Ireland

Acknowledgements

This has been a group effort in which each of us has played a part to the full: Bridget Cass as untiring coordinator; Mervyn Kohler, the fund-holder, who brought his promotional skills; Judith Stone, who invested unstinting energy to ensure that the anthology reflects family relationships in all their stages and diversities, and her colleagues, Karen Shoop and Amrita Narain, whose practical skills provided essential support; Judith Chernaik, who insisted that the poems were of the best; and James Berry, whose gentle encouragement maintained our dedication to the project throughout.

For suggesting the poems and shaping the anthology we are indebted to all those who sent in their favourite poems. We would also like to thank all the radio programmes which encouraged their listeners to contribute to the project. Without their contribution, the support of the European Union, which enabled us to broaden the project to include Laura Fargher from Ireland, Ernst van Altena, Ger Tielen and Johan Snel from the Netherlands, and the commitment of BBC Educational Developments, this anthology would have remained a dream.

The United Nations International Year of the Family has prompted greater family friendliness; we trust that this book will bring pleasure over many years.

Carolyn Douglas
Chair of Family Relations Group UK
November 1994

For further copies of this book, please send a cheque or postal order for £6.99 per copy, payable to BBC Education, to: Reflecting Families PO Box 7, London W3 6XJ

Judi Benson - 'Windy's House' - unpublished, printed by permission of the author

James Berry - 'Nana Krishie the Midwife' from *Chain of Days* (OUP 1985), reprinted by permission of the author

Sujata Bhatt - 'For My Grandmother' from *Brunizem* (Carcanet 1988) reprinted by permission of the publisher

Valerie Bloom - 'Chicken-poxed', & 'Granny' both unpublished; & 'Guidance' from *Duppy Jamboree* (CUP 1992) reprinted by permission of the author

• Eavan Boland - 'Night Feed' - from *Night Feed* (Arlen House 1982) reprinted by permission of the author

• Dermot Bolger - 'Holotropic Botanicus' from *Holotropic Botanicus* (New Island Books 1995) reprinted by permission of the publisher

Charles Causley - 'What has Happened to Lulu' from *Collected Poems 1951 - 1975* (Macmillan 1975) reprinted by permission of the publisher

Gillian Clarke - 'Shawl' from *Letting in the Rumans* (Carcanet 1989); and 'My Box', from *Selected Poems* (Carcanet 1985) reprinted by permission of the author

David Constantine - 'Suddenly she is radiant' from *Selected Poems*, (Bloodaxe Books 1991) reprinted by permission of the publisher

Wendy Cope - 'Sisters' from *Is That the New Moon?* first published 1979; 'The Baby of the Family' from *Casting a Spell* first published 1991 reprinted by permission of the author

Kevin Crossley-Holland - 'Naming You' from *New and Selected Poems* (Hutchinson 1991), reprinted by permission of Rogers Coleridge and White

Fred D'Aguiar - 'Granny on Her Singer Sewing Machine' from *British Subjects* (Bloodaxe Books 1993) reprinted by permission of the publisher

David Dabydeen - 'Catching Crabs' from *Turner: New and Selected Poems* (Jonathan Cape 1990) reprinted by permission of the author

Cecil Day Lewis - 'Walking Away' published in *Collected Poems* reprinted by permission of the Roger Cazlet

• John F Deane - 'Love' from *Walking in Water* (*Dedalus Press* 1994) reprinted by permission of the author

Maura Dooley - 'Mansize' *from Exploring Magnetism* (Bloodaxe Books 1991) reprinted by permission of the author

Carol Ann Duffy - 'The Way My Mother Speaks' from *The other Country* (Anvil Press Poetry 1990) reprinted by permission of the publisher

• Sean Dunne - 'The Smell of Cake'; 'Grandparents'- both published in *Against the Storm* (Dolmer Press 1986) reprinted by permission of Colin Smythe Ltd

• Paul Durcan - 'Stellar Manipulator' from *Daddy, Daddy*, (Blackstaff Press 1990) reprinted by permission of the publisher

T. S. Eliot - 'A Dedication to My Wife', published in *Collected Poems* (Faber) reprinted by permission of the publisher

Alistair Elliot - 'To A Son in the Middle East' from *My Country* (Carcanet 1989); 'The Cord' from *Turning the Stones* (Carcanet 1993) reprinted by permission of the publisher

Ruth Fainlight - 'Lineage' from *This Time of Year* (Sinclair Stevenson 1994) reprinted by permission of the publisher

U. A. Fanthorpe - 'Dumb Show' from *Neck-Verse* (Peterloo Poets, 1992) reprinted by permission of the publisher

Vicki Feaver - 'Slow Reader' from *Close Relatives* (Secker 1981) reprinted by permission of the author

John Fuller - 'Nant Gwtheyrn' from *The Mountain in the Sea* (Secker & Warburg 1975) reprinted by permission of the author

Lorna Goodison - 'I am becoming my mother' from *I am Becoming My Mother* (New Beacon Press 1986) reprinted by permission of the publisher

John Greening - 'Seven Sea Interludes' - first published in *Poetry Review* (Summer 1988) reprinted by permission of the author

Luuc Gruwez 'West Flanders' - from *in Maatstaf*, De Arbeiderspers, Singel 262, 1016 AC, Amsterdam, Holland.Translation Myra Scholz

Thom Gunn - 'First Meeting with a Possible Mother-in Law' published in *Collected Poems* (Faber 1993) reprinted by permission of the publisher

Michael Hamburger - 'For a Family Album' from *Collected Poems, 1941 - 1994*, (Anvil Press 1994) reprinted by permission of the author and publisher

Tony Harrison - 'Background Material' from *Continuous* (Rex Collins 1981) reprinted by permission of the author

• Seamus Heaney - 'Follower' from *New Selected Poems 1966 - 1987* (Faber, 1990); 'The Underground' published in *Station Island* (Faber) reprinted by permission of the publisher

Paul Henry - 'A634 NKX' from *Oxford Poetry* reprinted by permission of Seren Books

Cicely Herbert - 'Making Poems' unpublished, printed by permission of the author

Selima Hill - 'Mother Stone' from *Trembling Hearts in the Bodies of Dogs - New and Selected Poems* (Bloodaxe 1994) reprinted by permission of the publisher

Elizabeth Jennings - 'One Flesh' - from *Collected Poems* (Carcanet 1986) reprinted by permission of the publisher

Jenny Joseph - Changes from *The Inland Sea* (Papier Mache Press 1989) reprinted by permission of the author

Sylvia Kantaris - 'First Day of Spring' from *Dirty Washing* (Bloodaxe Books 1989) reprinted by permission of the author

• Patrick Kavanagh - 'In Memory of My Mother' from *Collected Poems* (Martin Brian and O'Keeffe 1964); 'Memory of My Father' from *The Complete Poems* (Peter Kavanagh 1972) reprinted by permission of the publishers

Jackie Kay - 'After Mammy Telt Me She Wasnie My Real Mammy', published in *The Adoption Papers* (Bloodaxe Books 1991) - 'Two of Everything' published in *Two's Company* (Puffin 1992) reprinted by permission of the publishers

Judith Kazantzis - 'The Separation' from *Let's Pretend* (Virago 1984) reprinted by permission of the author

Stephen Knight - 'Theresa' from *Flowering Limbs* (Bloodaxe Books 1993) reprinted by permission of the publisher

Philip Larkin - 'This be the Verse' *from High Windows* (Faber 1974) reprinted by permission of the publisher

• Anne Le Marquand Hartigan - 'Writing' from *Long Tongue* (Beaver Row Press 1982) reprinted by permission of the author

Liz Lochhead - 'Poem for My sister' from *Dreaming Frankenstein* (Polygon 1984) reprinted by permission of the publisher

Norman MacCaig - 'Aunt Julia' - *Collected Poems* (Chatto & Windus) reprinted by permission of the publisher

• Roger McGough - 'Sad Aunt Madge' from *The Mersey Sound* (Penguin 1967) reprinted by permission of Peters, Fraser and Dunlop

Medbh McGuckian - 'My Aunts' from *The Flower Master and other Poems* (The Gallery Press 1993) reprinted by permission of the author and publisher

Gerda Mayer - 'Make Believe' from *The Uprooted* (Plenum Press, 1993) © Gerda Mayer reprinted by permission of the author

Josephine Miles - 'Family' © Josephine Miles 1983, used with permission of the University of Illinois Press

Adrian Mitchell - 'Beatrix Is Three' from *Adrian Mitchell's Greatest Hits - The Top 40* (Bloodaxe Books). None of Adrian Mitchell's poems are to be used in connection with any examination whatsoever

John Mole - 'Going On' published in *Depending on the Light* (Peterloo Poets 1993) reprinted by permission of the author

Edwin Morgan - 'An Addition to the Family' from *Collected Poems* (Carcanet Press) reprinted by permission of the publisher

Grace Nichols - 'Praise Song for my Mother' from *The Fat Black Woman's Poems* (Virago 1984); 'Granny, Granny Please Comb My Hair' from *Lazy Thoughts of a Lazy Woman* (Virago 1989) reprinted by permission of the publisher

• Dennis O'Driscoll - 'Siblings United' from *Long Story Short* (Anvil Press Poetry/Dedalus Press 1993); and 'Siblings Revisited' from *Hidden Extras* (Anvil Press Poetry/Dedalus Press 1987) reprinted by permission of the author

Brian Patten - 'Looking for Dad' - from *Gargling With Jelly* (Penguin Poetry) reprinted by permission of Rogers, Coleridge & White

Sylvia Plath - 'Child' published in *Collected Poems* (Faber) reprinted by permission of the publisher

Peter Porter - 'Old Fashioned Wedding' from *The Cost of Seriousness* (OUP 1978) reprinted by permission of the publisher

Sheenagh Pugh - 'Old Widowers' from *Selected Poems* (Seren Books 1990) reprinted by permission of the author

Peter Redgrove - 'Memorial' from *The Moon Disposes*, (Secker & Warburg) reprinted by permission of David Higham Associates

Theodore Roethke - 'My Papa's Waltz' reprinted by permission of Faber & Faber

Andrew Salkey - 'My Grandmother' unpublished reprinted by permission of the author

Carole Satyamurti - 'Broken Moon' from *Broken Moon* (OUP 1987) reprinted by permission of the publisher

Vernon Scannell - 'Jane at Play' from *Collected Poems 1950 - 1993* (Robson Books 1994) reprinted by permission of the author

Penelope Shuttle - 'Outgrown' reprinted by permission of the author

Ruth Silcock - 'The Widower' from *Mrs Carmichael* (Anvil Press Poetry 1987) reprinted by permission of the publisher

Jon Silkin - 'Death of a Son' from S*elected Poems* (Sinclair-Stevenson) reprinted by permission of the publisher

Matt Simpson - 'Vacation Jobs' from *An Elegy for the Galosherman - New and Collected Poems* (Bloodaxe 1990) reprinted by permission of the publisher

Stevie Smith - 'A House of Mercy' from *The Collected Poems of Stevie Smith* (Penguin 20th Century Classics) by permission of James MacGibbon

Stephen Spender - 'To my Daughter' from *Collected Poems* (Faber) reprinted by permission of the publisher

Anne Stevenson - 'When the Camel is dust' from *Four and a Half Dancing Men* (OUP 1993); 'The Marriage' from *Selected Poems* (OUP 1987) reprinted by permission of the publisher

Anthony Thwaite - 'Jack' from *Poems 1953 - 1988* (Hutchinson 1989) reprinted by permission of the author

Charles Tomlinson - 'To my Daughter', 'After Hugo' from *The Hudson Review* 1994 reprinted by permission of the author

Willem van Toorn - 'Family' from *De Tweed Ronde*, 1983, Willem van Toorn, Frans van Mierisstraat 73 1071 RM Amsterdam

Derek Walcott - 'Love after Love' from *Collected Poems* (Faber 1986) reprinted by permission of the publisher

Susan Wicks - 'Virtuoso' - unpublished, printed by permission of the author

Hugo Williams - 'Now that I hear Trains' from *Writing Home* (OUP 1985) reprinted by permission of the publisher

David Wright - 'Balloon' *from Selected Poems* (Carcanet 1988) reprinted by permission of the publisher

Judith Wright - 'Request to a Year' from *Selected Poems* reprinted by permission of Angus and Robertson

• Kit Wright - 'Grandad' from *Rabbiting On* (HarperCollins 1978) reprinted by permission of the publisher

• Irish poets and poets selected by people living in the Republic of Ireland